AF228616

PHOENIX SUNS

BY PATRICK DONNELLY

SportsZone

An Imprint of Abdo Publishing
abdobooks.com

abdobooks.com

Published by Abdo Publishing, a division of ABDO, PO Box 398166, Minneapolis, Minnesota 55439. Copyright © 2023 by Abdo Consulting Group, Inc. International copyrights reserved in all countries. No part of this book may be reproduced in any form without written permission from the publisher. SportsZone™ is a trademark and logo of Abdo Publishing.

Printed in China
052022
092022

Cover Photo: Rick Scuteri/AP Images
Interior Photos: Melinda Nagy/Shutterstock Images, 1; Hannah Foslien/Getty Images Sport/Getty Images, 4; Christian Peterson/Getty Images Sport/Getty Images, 7, 8, 9; Harry How/Getty Images Sport/Getty Images, 11; Focus on Sport/Getty Images Sport/ Getty Images, 12, 15, 17, 27, 34; Icon Sportswire/Getty Images, 19; Jeff Gross/Getty Images Sport/Getty Images, 20; Kevork Djansezian/Getty Images Sport/Getty Images, 21; Focus on Sport/Getty Images, 22; Robert Kradin/AP Images, 25; Otto Greule Jr./ Hulton Archive/Getty Images, 28; Ronald Martinez/Getty Images Sport/Getty Images, 30; Jonathan Bachman/Getty Images Sport/Getty Images, 33; Bill Brett/Boston Globe/Getty Images, 36; Frank Leonhardt/Picture Alliance/Getty Images, 38; Brian Bahr/Getty Images Sport/Getty Images, 40; Elise Amendola/AP Images, 41

Editor: Charlie Beattie
Series Designer: Joshua Olson

Library of Congress Control Number: 2021951664

Publisher's Cataloging-in-Publication Data

Names: Donnelly, Patrick, author.
Title: Phoenix Suns / by Patrick Donnelly
Description: Minneapolis, Minnesota: Abdo Publishing, 2023 | Series: Inside the NBA |
    Includes online resources and index.
Identifiers: ISBN 9781532198410 (lib. bdg.) | ISBN 9781098272067 (ebook)
Subjects: LCSH: Phoenix Suns (Basketball team)--Juvenile literature. | Basketball--Juvenile
    literature. |
Professional sports--Juvenile literature. | Sports franchises--Juvenile literature.
Classification: DDC 796.32364--dc23

TABLE OF CONTENTS

CHAPTER ONE

PAUL PROVIDES

Chris Paul stood in disbelief on the Staples Center court in Los Angeles. His emotions surged as he tried to grasp what he had just accomplished. Going into the 2021 National Basketball Association (NBA) playoffs, Paul had long since established himself as one of the game's great point guards. Yet he was also known as one of the greatest players in NBA history never to have played in the Finals. All of that was about to change.

In 2010–11 the Suns began a stretch of 10 consecutive seasons missing the playoffs. Along the way, though, they began putting together a talented roster. In 2015 they drafted guard Devin Booker in the middle of the first round. Three years later, they won the NBA Draft lottery. They used the first pick of the draft to select center Deandre Ayton. And in November 2020, they traded for Paul.

The addition of Chris Paul before the 2020–21 season helped make the Suns an NBA championship contender.

The Suns' 10-year stretch of missing the playoffs was not without some bad luck. In 2013–14 Phoenix finished 48–34. Had they played in the Eastern Conference, the Suns would have been the third overall seed. But in the loaded West, Phoenix missed the playoffs completely. The Suns joined the 2007–08 Golden State Warriors as the only NBA teams to win 48 games and miss the postseason since the league had switched to a 16-team playoff format.

The veteran point guard proved to be the final piece of their playoff roster. The Suns won nine out of 10 games in mid-February. Their record surged to 20–10. They won six of their next eight to climb to second place in the West. And a 14–2 stretch that began in late March made them a true threat to overtake the Utah Jazz for the top spot in the conference.

They were a fun team to watch too. Booker had developed into one of the NBA's most consistent scorers. He could drive to the hoop or make teams pay by stepping back to hit three-pointers. Ayton was a double-double machine. He also protected the rim with his 6-foot-11-inch frame. And the 35-year-old Paul did more than just mentor his young teammates. He also averaged 16.4 points and 8.9 assists per game while leading the NBA in free-throw percentage.

Phoenix finished 51–21, one game behind the Jazz. But earning the number two seed meant they would be favorites in at least their first two playoff series. Then the Suns went out and proved their first playoff berth in a decade wasn't a fluke. They took down the Los Angeles Lakers in six games in the first round. Then they swept the Denver Nuggets to reach the conference finals.

CLIPPING LOS ANGELES

Devin Booker soars for a dunk during the Suns' second-round sweep of the Denver Nuggets.

The Suns didn't get a chance to face the top-seeded Jazz. That's because the other Los Angeles team had already knocked them out of the playoffs. The fourth-seeded Clippers upset Utah in the second round. Now the Suns were suddenly the favorite in the upcoming series.

Phoenix embraced its home-court advantage and came out firing. Booker exploded for 40 points in Game 1. That total was part of a triple-double that included 13 rebounds and 11 assists. Phoenix won 120–114. Cameron Payne led the way with 29 points in Game 2. But the Suns needed a last-second alley-oop from Jae Crowder to Ayton to pull out a one-point victory.

A last-second dunk from Deandre Ayton, *top right*, secured a victory for the Suns in Game 2 against the Clippers.

What made those wins even more impressive was that the Suns succeeded without Paul. He missed the games due to the NBA's COVID-19 health and safety protocols. But he was back in the lineup for Game 3. Paul had played with the Clippers from 2011 to 2017 and led them to some huge victories. Now it was time for him to turn the tables on his old club.

Los Angeles wasn't about to go down without a fight. The Clippers won two of the next three games. That included a 14-point road win in Game 5 that forced the series back to Los Angeles. The Suns had to win Game 6 in front of the Clippers' fans if they wanted to avoid a winner-take-all Game 7.

Paul got them off to a quick start. He hit consecutive three-pointers to give the Suns a 15–9 lead midway through the first quarter. Ayton played a big role with an early scoring surge as well. He hit a short jump hook, made a twisting move for a layup in traffic, and tipped in an alley-oop pass from

Booker, *left*, averaged 25.5 points per game during the 2021 Western Conference finals.

Booker. And Booker made three out of his last four shots in the quarter. The Suns took a 33–29 lead into the second.

Phoenix kept getting contributions from its entire lineup. Forward Dario Šarić came off the bench to hit two straight three-pointers. That helped Phoenix stretch its lead to double digits early in the second. Then, after the Clippers rallied to tie the score 50–50, Crowder took over. Ayton grabbed an offensive rebound and found him open in the corner for a huge three-pointer to regain the lead. Crowder hit two more triples down the stretch. He scored 13 of the Suns' last 16 points before halftime.

KNOCKOUT PUNCH

One more strong half was all Phoenix needed to reach the NBA Finals for the first time since 1993. Paul was on a mission to make it happen. He began the third quarter by hitting an 18-foot jumper. He fed Ayton and forward Mikal Bridges for layups. With 4:01 left in the third, Phoenix was pulling away, leading 89–72.

Then the Clippers went on a 10–0 run to cut the lead to seven. Los Angeles was known as a comeback team. They had just overcome a 25-point deficit to beat the Jazz in Game 6 of the previous round.

Paul made sure that didn't happen again. He answered the 10–0 run with a three-pointer. Then he drove to the hoop for a layup in traffic. Another three-pointer followed with nine seconds left in the third quarter. Eight straight points from Paul took the wind out of the Clippers' sails.

But he was far from done with his epic night. Early in the fourth, Paul hit three straight shots. One of them came after a baseline drive that took him under the hoop. He dribbled behind his back to fake out a defender, then turned around and hit a wide-open 10-footer.

Next, Paul's pull-up jumper from 18 feet put the Suns up by 20 points. And he kept shooting. Paul hit a step-back

Chris Paul holds up the Western Conference championship trophy after the Suns' Game 6 victory over the Clippers.

three-pointer and drew a foul to make it a four-point play. A pull-up three expanded the lead to 118–92.

Finally, with 2:20 to play, Paul launched one last long-range shot. It found nothing but net. He flipped the bottom of his jersey free from his waistband as if to say to the Suns' sideline, "My work here is done." Phoenix coach Monty Williams pulled him from the game with 2:01 left. Paul stood near the bench, yelling to the noisy Suns fans who had made the trip from Phoenix.

He had plenty of reason to shout. Paul had scored 31 of his game-high 41 points in the second half. He was on the way to the NBA Finals for the first time. And his Suns would play for a title for the first time in 28 years.

DESERT HOOPS

During its first decade, the NBA was composed of teams from the eastern and midwestern parts of the United States. Then the Minneapolis Lakers moved to Los Angeles in 1960. Two years later, the Warriors left Philadelphia for San Francisco. Suddenly the NBA had visions of becoming a truly national league.

Phoenix was hardly a big city in those days. The population of the Phoenix area in 1965 was just under 700,000. But the American Southwest was growing, and Phoenix was the center of that trend.

City leaders knew that adding major league sports would help make Phoenix more attractive to businesses and tourists. But most of their efforts centered on landing a pro football team. Richard L. Bloch, a local real estate developer, had

Alvan Adams, *center*, played a team-record 988 games for the Suns before retiring in 1988.

other ideas. He was a basketball fan and thought Phoenix would be a good fit for the NBA.

It took some convincing, but Bloch had geography on his side. The league had added teams in Seattle and San Diego in 1967. And it was fighting off a challenge from a new rival league, the American Basketball Association (ABA). The NBA didn't want the ABA to gain a foothold in any potential NBA markets. So in January 1968, the league announced it had granted expansion franchises to Milwaukee and Phoenix.

BUILDING THE SUNS

One of the Suns' first moves was to hire 28-year-old Jerry Colangelo as the team's general manager. Colangelo was a highly regarded scouting director for the Chicago Bulls. He brought Bulls head coach Red Kerr with him to fill the same role in Phoenix.

It was a logical move for a new NBA team. Two years earlier, the Bulls had been an expansion team. Colangelo helped build their first roster, and Kerr coached them to a playoff berth. Now they were tasked with the same job in Phoenix.

Curtis Perry, *left*, averaged a double-double during his first season with the Suns in 1974–75.

The two had a tougher job in the desert. The addition of five new teams in just three years had thinned out the league's talent pool. And the creation of the ABA in 1967 made building a roster even more difficult. The Suns decided to focus on developing young players with high potential rather than playing journeyman veterans who might help them win a few extra games right away. Reserve guard Bob Warlick, just 27 years old, was their oldest player that first season.

They did have a handful of future stars. Point guard Gail Goodrich came over from the Lakers in the expansion draft. He led the team by averaging 23.8 points and 6.4 assists per game in its first season. Former Knicks guard Dick Van Arsdale checked in at 21.0 points and 6.9 rebounds. Both players represented the Suns at the All-Star Game.

However, that first Suns team struggled on the court. They finished just 16–66, the worst record in the NBA that season. When they started slowly the next season, Colangelo fired Kerr and took over on the bench for the rest of the year. The move worked. The Suns improved to 39–43 and made the playoffs. They even took a 3–1 lead over the heavily favored Lakers in their first-round playoff series, but Los Angeles rallied to win three straight and advance.

The next two seasons were even more fruitful. Under new head coach Cotton Fitzsimmons, the Suns went 48–34 in 1970–71. The next season they were 49–33. However, they were left out of the playoffs both years. In those days, the league was split into four divisions. The top two teams from each division qualified for the postseason. And the Suns were stuck behind two of the league's best teams—the Bucks and the Bulls.

ESTABLISHING A WINNER

Fitzsimmons took off to coach the Atlanta Hawks after two seasons. A year later, Colangelo hired the most successful head coach in team history. John MacLeod led the Suns to the playoffs nine times over the next 14 seasons. No coach has had a longer career in Phoenix.

John MacLeod, *right*, won 579 games as head coach of the Suns. It helped being able to coach players like six-time All-Star Walter Davis, *left*.

The highlight of the MacLeod years came in 1975–76. The Suns finished 42–40 and reached the playoffs for the first time since their surprising battle with the Lakers five years earlier. What followed was even more surprising. Seeded third in the Western Conference, the Suns upset the second-seeded Seattle SuperSonics in six games to advance to the conference finals. Then they shocked the top-seeded Golden State Warriors in seven games. Phoenix finally met its match in the NBA Finals against the mighty Boston Celtics. But the Suns took the series to six games before bowing out.

The Suns got back to the conference finals in 1979 and 1984 but got no further. Fitzsimmons returned in 1988 and led the team to the Western Conference finals in his first two seasons back in Phoenix. But he was no more successful than MacLeod at getting the team over the hump. The Suns were developing the reputation of a team that teased fans with big promise but couldn't win in the playoffs.

That changed in 1993. Paul Westphal, a key member of the late-1970s Suns playoff teams, had spent four years as an assistant coach under Fitzsimmons. Westphal was elevated to head coach before the 1992–93 season, and the Suns went on a run. Newly acquired forward Charles Barkley led a deep, balanced roster to 62 victories. That was both the best record in the NBA that season and the best in Suns history to that point.

That record earned Phoenix the top seed in the Western Conference, but the team wouldn't have an easy path to the NBA Finals. The Lakers pushed Phoenix to the limit in the opening round. Then the Suns needed seven games to knock

Charles Barkley backs down a Boston Celtics defender during a 1993 game.

out Seattle in the conference finals. But the Suns survived, reaching the NBA Finals for the first time since 1976. They lost to the two-time defending champion Bulls in six games, but the future looked bright in Phoenix.

Amar'e Stoudemire (1) averaged more than 20 points per game five times in eight years for the Suns after the team drafted him in 2002.

OUT OF THE DESERT

A series of promising regular seasons and playoff flops followed for the next decade. Fitzsimmons even replaced Westphal halfway through the 1995–96 season. He lasted less than a year before the team hired former guard Danny Ainge. But no one could get the Suns out of the second round in the postseason.

The Suns finally seemed to find the right formula in 2004–05. Second-year head coach Mike D'Antoni installed an up-tempo system that suited his team's talent. Point guard Steve Nash, center Amar'e Stoudemire, and forward Shawn Marion thrived in the Suns' breakneck style of play. They won five playoff series in three years under D'Antoni. But like Phoenix teams of the past, they couldn't finish the job.

Nash and Stoudemire led one more run to the conference finals in 2010. But then came a 10-year playoff drought.

Chris Paul (3) shoots over a pair of Los Angeles Lakers during the opening round of the 2021 playoffs.

Talented guard Devin Booker arrived to energize the franchise in 2015. The addition of center Deandre Ayton and point guard Chris Paul helped the Suns reach the NBA Finals in 2021. Despite a Finals loss to the Bucks, Phoenix looked set as a championship contender for years to come.

CHAPTER THREE

STAR SUNS

Like most expansion teams, the Suns didn't start out with a lot of talent. However, their first roster did include the player who would become known as "the Original Sun." Dick Van Arsdale spent his first three NBA seasons with the New York Knicks. Then Phoenix selected him in the expansion draft.

Van Arsdale scored the first points in team history with a layup against the Seattle SuperSonics. He quickly became a fixture in the Suns lineup. The guard averaged 42.4 minutes per game in his first season in Phoenix. He also averaged more than 21 points per game in each of his first three seasons in the desert.

Van Arsdale lasted long enough to help the Suns reach the NBA Finals in 1976 before retiring the next year. He returned to coach the team briefly in 1987, taking over for the man who once coached him in Phoenix, John MacLeod.

Dick Van Arsdale scored more than 12,000 points in nine seasons with the Suns.

In their second season, the Suns signed Connie Hawkins. The high-flying forward was already 26 years old, but he had never played in the NBA. Hawkins was kicked out of the University of Iowa in 1961 when he was accused of gambling on college sports. Even though Hawkins was innocent, he still was not drafted by an NBA team when he became eligible three years later. Despite being known for his elite athleticism, Hawkins looked like he might never get the chance to show his skills in the country's best league. After spending a few years with the Harlem Globetrotters, he signed with the ABA and spent two years lighting up scoreboards. While playing in the rival league, Hawkins sued the NBA for keeping him out. The league finally let up and allowed him to sign with the Suns.

Hawkins wasted no time. He averaged 20.5 points and 9.0 rebounds per game in his four full years with the Suns. An All-Star each of those seasons, Hawkins was the Suns'

Forward Connie Hawkins was one of the Suns' earliest stars.

leading scorer when they took the Lakers to seven games in their first playoff series.

BURNING BRIGHT

Before the 1975–76 season, the Suns made two key acquisitions that put them on the road to the NBA Finals. First, they traded high-scoring point guard Charlie Scott to the Boston Celtics for shooting guard Paul Westphal. The 25-year-old Westphal had come off the bench for the Celtics. He played a key defensive role in their run to the 1974 NBA title. But he blossomed in Phoenix, where he became a three-time All-NBA first-team selection for his dynamic all-around game.

The Suns also selected University of Oklahoma center Alvan Adams with the fourth pick in that year's draft. Adams spent the next 13 seasons anchoring the middle of the Phoenix lineup. He earned his sole All-Star Game selection during his rookie season. That year he averaged a career-high 19.0 points and added 9.1 rebounds per game.

The Suns didn't reach the NBA Finals again for 17 years, but they still had plenty of quality players along the way. One was swingman Walter Davis, who was the fifth pick of the 1977 draft. Davis won the NBA Rookie of the Year Award when he averaged 24.2 points that season. The six-time All-Star spent 11 years in Phoenix and remains the franchise's all-time leading scorer. The team ended up retiring Davis's No. 6 jersey and adding him to its Ring of Honor.

SIR CHARLES AND HIS COURT

Kevin Johnson was a backup point guard for the Cleveland Cavaliers in 1987–88. Behind All-Star Mark Price, he wasn't seeing much playing time. But a trade that year brought him to Phoenix. It kick-started Johnson's career. It also started Phoenix's ball rolling toward an appearance in the 1993 NBA

Kevin Johnson started a trend of excellent Phoenix point guards when he joined the Suns in 1988.

Finals. The quick point guard spent the rest of his career with the Suns and earned three All-Star nods. Over a four-year span that started in 1988–89, Johnson averaged 21.2 points and 11.1 assists.

Johnson's backcourt mate on the 1993 Finals team was Dan Majerle. "Thunder Dan" was a dangerous three-point

Jason Kidd led the Suns to the playoffs in each of his four full seasons with the team.

shooter and a strong defender. But he got his nickname for his high-flying dunks that would energize the crowd at Suns home games.

Two veteran forwards also played important roles on that Western Conference championship team. Tom Chambers made three of his four All-Star teams while playing in Phoenix. But by the 1993 season, the 33-year-old had accepted a role as the team's sixth man. He averaged 20.4 points and 6.6 rebounds per game in his five seasons with the Suns.

The biggest personality on the team was Charles Barkley. The brash forward came over in a trade with the Philadelphia 76ers before the 1992–93 season. In his eight NBA seasons, he had developed a reputation as one of the game's best rebounders—and biggest talkers. Barkley's mouth sometimes got him in trouble. But his play often bailed out the Suns. In 1992–93 he was at his best. "Sir Charles" averaged 25.6 points per game and 12.2 rebounds. At the end of the season, he was named the NBA's Most Valuable Player (MVP). Barkley lasted three more seasons in Phoenix, and he was an All-Star in each one of them.

MODERN SUNS

Jason Kidd was another future Hall of Famer who passed through Phoenix. The Suns traded for the 23-year-old point

Steve Nash, *left*, and Shawn Marion, *right*, were keys to the Suns' success in the 2000s.

guard in December 1996. In his four full seasons in the desert, Kidd led the NBA in assists three times.

Kidd was joined in the Hall of Fame by fellow point guard Steve Nash. A native of South Africa who grew up in Canada, Nash was the Suns' first-round pick in the 1996 draft. But he was stuck behind Kidd for the first two seasons of his career. Phoenix then traded him to Dallas, where he blossomed into an All-Star.

Nash returned to the Suns as a free agent in 2004 and was the engine driving the fast-paced Suns offense for the next eight seasons. He led the NBA in assists five times while remaining a consistent scorer and one of the best free-throw shooters in league history.

Nash thrived under head coach Mike D'Antoni's up-tempo style. D'Antoni pushed players to shoot early and often, especially from the three-point range. The Suns led the NBA in three-pointers in 2004–05. One of the stars of that system was Shawn Marion. The forward averaged 20.6 points and 11.6 rebounds per game over Nash's first two seasons back with the Suns.

Meanwhile, big man Amar'e Stoudemire took advantage of the space created by the Suns' shooters to dominate inside. In 2004–05 the third-year center averaged a career-high 26.0 points while earning the first of his six All-Star berths. Stoudemire was also a reliable rebounder and shot-blocker. The 6-foot-10-inch Stoudemire broke out in the 2005 Western Conference finals. He averaged 37.0 points and 9.8 rebounds in the series.

BOOK IT

Devin Booker didn't make waves when he was drafted thirteenth overall in 2015. After all, three other players on his University of Kentucky team were drafted above him.

Booker was known as a good shooter in college. But many wondered if he would ever be more than that in the NBA. He quickly proved doubters wrong.

The young guard averaged 22.1 points per game in just his second season. He did it showcasing not only a good shot but also a natural feel for all aspects of the offensive game. Booker developed into a star over the next few seasons, even while the team struggled around him.

Joining Booker in 2018 was center Deandre Ayton. Unlike Booker, Ayton arrived in the NBA with all the hype that normally follows the top overall pick in the draft. And the 6-foot-11-inch, 250-pound center lived up to It from day one. He averaged a double-double in his first season. A year later, he helped the Suns improve from 19 to 34 wins.

The final piece to the puzzle came in November 2020. Chris Paul had been an elite point guard in the NBA since 2005. Now 35 years old, he formed a deadly backcourt duo with Booker. The results were immediate. The Suns fell one game short of the NBA's best record and reached the NBA Finals. Booker, Ayton, and Paul fell in six games to the Milwaukee Bucks. But it was just the beginning for the trio in Phoenix. They returned the next season as one of the NBA's favorites to win it all.

Deandre Ayton (22) played college basketball at the University of Arizona before the Suns selected him first overall in 2018.

CHAPTER FOUR

MAKING MEMORIES

The 1976 NBA Finals were supposed to be a mismatch. The Boston Celtics had already won 12 NBA titles entering that season. The Suns hadn't even been around for a decade. And they had made the playoffs only once before.

Game 5 of the series was one of the craziest games in NBA history. The Celtics raced to a 20-point lead in the first quarter. But the Suns kept their composure and climbed back into the game, eventually forcing overtime. One overtime period wasn't enough to decide it. Late in the second overtime, the Suns scored twice in the final 15 seconds to take a one-point lead.

That was plenty of time for the Celtics. Boston forward John Havlicek took the inbounds pass from midcourt and drove to the basket. His bank shot from the side of the lane went in. The horn sounded, and fans swarmed the Boston Garden court, thinking the Celtics had pulled out a 111–110 victory.

Paul Westphal helped lead the Suns into the 1976 NBA Finals against his former team, the Boston Celtics.

Gar Heard (24) played a game-high 61 minutes during the triple-overtime NBA Finals game between the Suns and Celtics in 1976.

But after a discussion, the officials agreed the clock should have stopped with one second remaining. The floor was cleared, and the Suns were allowed to inbound the ball under their own basket. Still, it would take a miracle for them to make another shot. But Westphal had a brilliant idea. He called a timeout, knowing the Suns had already used all their timeouts. The penalty for that technical foul was one free throw for the Celtics, which they made.

However, Westphal knew that by rule, the Suns would now get to inbound the ball from midcourt. Curtis Perry passed it to Gar Heard at the top of the key. Heard had time to turn around and launch a high-arcing shot that splashed through the hoop, tying the game 112–112.

The exhausted players carried on. This time, the Celtics pulled ahead to stay, winning 128–126. The triple-overtime thriller has been called the greatest game ever played.

BARKLEY STEPS UP

The Suns were looking for a star when they traded for Charles Barkley in 1992. They got an MVP. And after winning the award during the regular season, Barkley was even better in the playoffs.

First he knocked out the San Antonio Spurs on a late shot in Game 6 of the second round. Barkley's 20-foot jumper over Spurs center David Robinson with one second left broke a 100–100 tie. Phoenix moved on

Another Triple Treat

Only once since the Suns and Celtics went to triple-overtime has an NBA Finals game lasted as long. And when it happened again, the Suns were also involved. Phoenix trailed the Chicago Bulls 2–0 heading into Game 3 in the 1993 Finals. Chicago was also playing at home. Bulls star Michael Jordan poured in 44 points. But seven Suns finished with double-figure scoring totals. Dan Majerle led the way with 28 points as the Suns outlasted Chicago 129–121.

Charles Barkley averaged 26.6 points and 13.6 rebounds during the Suns' 1993 playoff run.

when center Oliver Miller blocked Robinson's attempt to tie the game at the buzzer.

That set the table for a thrilling seven-game series with the Seattle SuperSonics. The teams traded wins through the first six games. And Barkley traded the spotlight with Seattle's star power forward, Shawn Kemp. In Game 6, Kemp garnered headlines with a 22-point, 15-rebound performance. Barkley's effort was not nearly as impressive. He had only 13 points.

However, with a trip to the Finals on the line, Barkley stormed out of the gate in Game 7. He posted an incredible stat line of 44 points and 24 rebounds. No player had put up 40 points and 20 rebounds in a Game 7 since 1962.

SEVEN SECONDS OR LESS

In the early 2000s, NBA games were slow, plodding affairs. Rugged defense kept scores low. But Phoenix coach Mike D'Antoni saw things differently. His "Seven Seconds or Less" offense was designed to get shots off quickly so other teams could not get back and slow things down.

In 2005 the Suns rode that fast pace to the Western Conference finals. But to get there, they had to win a tough series against the Dallas Mavericks in the second round. After five high-scoring games, the teams played out an epic overtime thriller in Game 6.

Phoenix rallied from a nine-point halftime deficit to force the extra session. Then point guard Steve Nash and forward Shawn Marion took over. The pair combined for

Steve Nash celebrates near the end of Phoenix's Game 6 victory over the Dallas Mavericks in 2005.

18 of Phoenix's 19 overtime points as the Suns outlasted Dallas 130–126.

On the night, Nash finished with 39 points, 12 assists, and nine rebounds. Marion had 38 points and 16 boards. Both players played Phoenix's up-tempo style for over 50 minutes in the game.

The Suns fell to the San Antonio Spurs in the West final. But D'Antoni's system helped bring fast-paced, high-scoring games back to the NBA.

BOOKER GOES OFF

In 1960 Los Angeles Lakers forward Elgin Baylor became the first player to score 70 points in a game. Until 2017 only four other players had ever done it—Wilt Chamberlain, David Thompson, David Robinson, and Kobe Bryant. Even the legendary Michael Jordan never topped the 70-point mark in his amazing career.

On March 24, 2017, 20-year-old Devin Booker added his name to that list. To make his feat even more impressive,

Devin Booker, *left*, drives for two of his 70 points against the Boston Celtics in March 2017.

Booker did most of his damage in just one half. The young guard had just 19 points at halftime. But in the third quarter he added 23 more. Sensing he was hot, Booker's teammates continued feeding him in the fourth. The result was 28 more points. He finished with exactly 70.

The record-setting night came in a 130–120 loss to the Boston Celtics. In fact, that defeat was part of a 13-game losing streak for the struggling Suns. But it was a sign that they had their first cornerstone in Booker. A few years later, he was pouring in points at the NBA Finals.

TIMELINE

1968

The NBA expands to 14 teams, adding new franchises in Phoenix and Milwaukee. The Phoenix entry is called the Suns, and they are the first major professional team in any sport to play in Arizona.

1969

The Suns lose a coin flip to the Milwaukee Bucks to determine the first pick of the upcoming NBA Draft. Milwaukee selects Kareem Abdul-Jabbar. With the second pick, Phoenix drafts center Neal Walk.

1970

The Suns finish 39–43 and reach the playoffs in their second season. They build a 3–1 series lead in the opening round against the powerhouse Los Angeles Lakers before losing in seven games.

1973

John MacLeod is hired as head coach. He leads the Suns for 14 seasons and posts a career record of 579–543 (.516).

1976

The Cinderella Suns upset the Seattle SuperSonics and Golden State Warriors to reach the NBA Finals, where they fall to the Boston Celtics in six games.

1979

Phoenix reaches the Western Conference finals, but the SuperSonics get revenge in a seven-game slugfest.

1984

The Suns finish 41–41 but knock off the Portland Trail Blazers and Utah Jazz to reach the conference finals, where they fall to the Lakers in six games.

1989

Cotton Fitzsimmons returns as head coach and leads the Suns to the Western Conference finals, but they are swept by the Lakers.

1990

The Suns return to the conference finals before falling to Portland in six games.

1992

Former Phoenix star Paul Westphal returns to coach the Suns, and the team trades for future Hall of Famer Charles Barkley.

1993

The Suns advance to the NBA Finals, but Michael Jordan and the Chicago Bulls eliminate them in a tense six-game series.

2004

Future Hall of Famer Steve Nash returns to the Suns six years after he was traded to the Dallas Mavericks.

2005

Head coach Mike D'Antoni, Nash, and center Amar'e Stoudemire lead the Suns to 62 wins, the best record in the NBA, but Phoenix falls to the San Antonio Spurs in the conference finals.

2007

The Suns win their third straight Pacific Division title, but they lose to San Antonio in the conference semifinals.

2010

Stoudemire, Nash, and second-year coach Alvin Gentry lead the Suns back to the Western Conference finals, where Kobe Bryant and the Lakers eliminate them in six games.

2015

Phoenix selects 18-year-old University of Kentucky guard Devin Booker with the thirteenth pick in the NBA Draft.

2021

Behind Booker, Chris Paul, and Deandre Ayton, the Suns reach the NBA Finals, where they take a 2–0 lead over the Bucks before losing in six games.

FRANCHISE HISTORY

Phoenix Suns (1968–)

KEY PLAYERS

Alvan Adams (1975–88)
Deandre Ayton (2018–)
Charles Barkley (1992–96)
Devin Booker (2015–)
Walter Davis (1977–88)
Kevin Johnson (1988–99, 2000)
Dan Majerle (1988–95,
   2001–02)
Shawn Marion (1999–2008)
Larry Nance (1981–88)
Steve Nash (1996–98, 2004–12)
Chris Paul (2020–)
Amar'e Stoudemire (2002–10)
Dick Van Arsdale (1968–77)
Paul Westphal (1975–80,
   1983–84)

KEY COACHES

Mike D'Antoni (2003–08)
Cotton Fitzsimmons (1970–72,
   1988–92, 1996)
John MacLeod (1973–87)

HOME ARENAS

Arizona Veterans Memorial
   Coliseum (1968–92)
Footprint Center (1992–)
   Formerly known as:
   America West Arena
      (1992–2006)
   US Airways Center (2006–15)
   Talking Stick Resort Arena
      (2015–20)
   PHX Arena (2020–21)
   Phoenix Suns Arena (2021)

TEAM
TRIVIA

NANCE TAKES HIS CHANCE

The NBA held its first dunk contest in 1984. The field included Dominique Wilkins, who was known as the "Human Highlight Film" for his dunking skills. It also included Julius Erving, who had won the first-ever dunk contest when the ABA held the event eight years earlier. But Suns forward Larry Nance upset the favorites to win the event. His 134 points just barely topped Erving's 132 in the finals.

NAME-BRAND PRIZE

Like many NBA teams, the Suns got their name from a fan contest. Phoenix resident Selinda King offered the winning suggestion. For her victory, King was given $1,000 and tickets to every Suns home game for their first season.

SMASHING THE SCOREBOARD

On November 10, 1990, the Suns defeated the Denver Nuggets 173–143. Phoenix scored 107 points in the first half, a record for most points in the first half of an NBA game. Forward Cedric Ceballos led the way with 32 points on 12-for-15 shooting.

HE'S STILL GOT IT

On April 9, 2019, Suns guard Jamal Crawford scored 51 points in a 120–109 loss to the Dallas Mavericks. At 39 years and 20 days old, Crawford was the oldest player to score at least 50 points in an NBA game.

alley-oop
A pass that is caught and immediately dunked before the shooter lands on the ground.

assist
A pass that leads directly to a basket.

berth
A spot in a competition or tournament earned through previous results.

double-double
Accumulating 10 or more of two certain statistics in a game.

draft
A system that allows teams to acquire new players coming into a league.

dynamic
Energetic and exciting; in sports, usually referring to an athlete with one or more outstanding skills.

expansion
The addition of new teams to increase the size of a league.

franchise
A sports organization, including the top-level team and all minor league affiliates.

layup
A shot made from close to the basket; an easy shot.

rebound
To catch the ball after a shot has been missed.

rookie
A professional athlete in his or her first year of competition.

sixth man
A key substitute for a basketball team; normally the first player to enter the game off the bench.

up-tempo
A fast pace of play.

veteran
A player who has played many years.

BOOKS

Flynn, Brendan. *The NBA Encyclopedia for Kids*. Minneapolis, MN: Abdo Publishing, 2022.

Graves, Will. *NBA*. Minneapolis, MN: Abdo Publishing, 2021.

Mason, Tyler. *Ultimate NBA Road Trip*. Minneapolis, MN: Abdo Publishing, 2019.

ONLINE RESOURCES

To learn more about the Phoenix Suns, please visit **abdobooklinks.com** or scan this QR code. These links are routinely monitored and updated to provide the most current information available.

INDEX

ABOUT THE AUTHOR

Patrick Donnelly is a freelance writer who lives in Minneapolis, Minnesota. He has covered the NBA for 20 years.